Intimacy

A 16-Day Devotional

Becoming a Close Friend of God

Discussing Intimacy, the Barriers, and the Types

Testimony Foreword

In 2009 I had been living in New York City for about 4 years with my husband and, at the time, our two children. I was away from my entire family and all that was "comfortable" to me. It would have been bearable if my husband and I were in sync... our marriage was hanging on by a thread. I was a wreck (mentally, physically, emotionally and spiritually); I was ready to give up on my marital union. Then a series of events occurred that tried to destroy me, I left my spouse and returned to Ohio.

While staying at my parents' home, my earthly father came to me and said, "Daughter, your mourning time is over. It was justifiable, yet now it is over. You must seek God and ask Him what to do and then make your decision. Whatever you decide, I will support." I was not ready to do this. Then my Dad said, "You have until Thursday." I remember being totally baffled and upset, how could the deadline be on Thursday when it was already Tuesday!

I thought about what my father said and I knew he was right. Yet it wasn't until Thursday came that I really began to seek God for direction. God showed me through His word and in a still small voice, my instructions... *Don't throw in the towel*. I went back to New York.

Even though things did not change overnight, I trusted God that my marriage would be what He promised. What did I do while waiting for my manifested promise? I allowed God to mold me into a better person, wife, and mother and I immersed myself in worship.

All the worship led to writing... That is how this devotional began. I longed to *Kiss the Face of God*, *Worship*. Later as I was teaching a class on Spiritual Gifts, the Intimacy work was created. Now the *Worship* and *Intimacy* writings have been combined for this Devotional.

Table of Contents

**YOU are ENCOURAGED to KEEP a DAILY JOURNAL

while READING this DEVOTIONAL**

Day 1 - *What is Intimacy?*

Intimacy – (noun) close familiarity or friendship

After reading the definition we must first understand that intimacy is not a verb, something you are doing at the moment. Intimacy is a noun, meaning it is the state of; therefore, Intimacy is not what you are doing, but who you are... Intimacy never stops, it is continuous.

Now we understand the importance of our subject's part of speech. What does intimacy mean in our culture? It is safe to say that intimacy is a human desire; real intimacy makes us feel alive, like we've been found. Someone finally took the time to peer into the depths of our soul and really see us.

However, no one can get to the depths of your soul in just a moment... *Intimacy is an ongoing process.*

How can we begin an intimate relationship with our Lord? How can we get and be so close with Him that our friendship and familiarity is continuous? Our Heavenly Father designed us in His image; therefore, how we create intimacy with our spouse or a close friend mirrors how we create an intimate relationship with Him. Our Lord has already called us His friend and is just waiting on us to seek Him and build this relationship with Him.

Scriptures

John 15:13-15 (KJV)

> *Greater love hath no man than this, that a man lay down his life for his friends. Ye are my friends, if ye do whatsoever I command you. Henceforth I call you not servants; for the servant knoweth not what his lord doeth: but I call you friends; for all things that I have heard of my Father I have made known unto you.*

Acts 17:27 (AMP)

So that they should seek God, in hope that they might feel after Him and find Him, although He is not far from us.

John 14:21 (AMP)

The person who has My commands and keeps them is the one who [really] loves Me; and whoever really loves Me will be loved by My Father, and I [too] will love him and will show (reveal, manifest) Myself to him. [I will let Myself be clearly seen by him and make Myself real to him.]

Prayer

Lord God, You are so Amazing! I Love You and Adore You. You chose me to be in relationship with You. I am so humbled and honored at Your love for me. I desire an intimate relationship with You. Your word says if I draw nigh to You, You will draw nigh to me. As we begin this journey of a closer walk with You, a more intimate process, allow me to obtain a greater understanding of You as My Lord and My Savior and My Friend. In Jesus Name, Amen.

Day 2 – *Intimacy Barrier Sin*

Barrier – an obstacle that prevents movement of access

Now we know that God desires for us to be his friend and in relationship with Him, but what is holding us back from entering into an intimate realm. What is blocking you?

Today we are going to deal with a huge barrier... Sin.

Let's consider a relationship that you have that means so much to you. If that person did something awful to you, or did something that you asked them not to do, or betrayed your trust... How would you treat that person? What if it was your spouse/someone you are in a serious relationship with, would you want them trying to show you affection after they wronged you? If it was a friend would you want to speak with them? Would you share your intimate thoughts with them again?

How do you think God feels? He asks us to keep His commandments... our behavior, our actions, our conversations... are they conducive to an "environment" that our Lord dwells in continuously?

Read the scriptures below then take some time to examine yourself. Are there things in your life that are obvious sins, secret sins, things God has told you to do that you have not done. Now is the time to repent, turn away.

Scriptures

Isaiah 59:2 (HCSB)
But your iniquities have been barriers between you and God, and your sins have made Him hide His face from you so that He does not listen.

Ephesians 5:1-21 (AMP)

Therefore become imitators of God [copy Him and follow His example], as well-beloved children [imitate their father]; ^{2} *and walk continually in love [that is, value one another—practice empathy and compassion, unselfishly seeking the best for others], just as Christ also loved you and gave Himself up for us, an offering and sacrifice to God [slain for you, so that it became] a sweet fragrance.*

^{3} *But sexual immorality and all [moral] impurity [indecent, offensive behavior] or greed must not even be hinted at among you, as is proper among saints [for as believers our way of life, whether in public or in private, reflects the validity of our faith].* ^{4} *Let there be no filthiness and silly talk, or coarse [obscene or vulgar] joking, because such things are not appropriate [for believers]; but instead speak of your thankfulness [to God].* ^{5} *For be sure of this: no immoral, impure, or greedy person—for that one is [in effect] an idolater—has any inheritance in the kingdom of Christ and God [for such a person places a higher value on something other than God].*

^{6} *Let no one deceive you with empty arguments [that encourage you to sin], for because of these things the wrath of God comes upon the sons of disobedience [those who habitually sin].* ^{7} *So do not participate or even associate with them [in the rebelliousness of sin].* ^{8} *For once you were darkness, but now you are Light in the Lord; walk as children of Light [live as those who are native-born to the Light]* ^{9} *(for the fruit [the effect, the result] of the Light consists in all goodness and righteousness and truth),* ^{10} *trying to learn [by experience] what is pleasing to the Lord [and letting your lifestyles be examples of what is most acceptable to Him—your behavior expressing gratitude to God for your salvation].* ^{11} *Do not participate in the worthless and unproductive deeds of darkness, but instead expose them [by exemplifying personal integrity, moral courage, and godly character];* ^{12} *for it is disgraceful even to mention the things that such people practice in secret.* ^{13} *But all things become visible when they are exposed by the light [of God's precepts], for it is light that makes everything visible.* ^{14} *For this reason He says, "Awake, sleeper,*

And arise from the dead, And Christ will shine [as dawn] upon you and give you light." [15] *Therefore see that you walk carefully [living life with honor, purpose, and courage; shunning those who tolerate and enable evil], not as the unwise, but as wise [sensible, intelligent, discerning people],* [16] *making the very most of your time [on earth, recognizing and taking advantage of each opportunity and using it with wisdom and diligence], because the days are [filled with] evil.* [17] *Therefore do not be foolish and thoughtless, but understand and firmly grasp what the will of the Lord is.* [18] *Do not get drunk with wine, for that is wickedness (corruption, stupidity), but be filled with the [Holy] Spirit and constantly guided by Him.* [19] *Speak to one another in psalms and hymns and spiritual songs, [offering praise by] singing and making melody with your heart to the Lord;* [20] *always giving thanks to God the Father for all things, in the name of our Lord Jesus Christ;* [21] *being subject to one another out of reverence for Christ.*

1 Corinthians 10:13 (AMP)

[12] *Therefore let the one who thinks he stands firm [immune to temptation, being overconfident and self-righteous], take care that he does not fall [into sin and condemnation].* [13] *No temptation [regardless of its source] has overtaken or enticed you that is not common to human experience [nor is any temptation unusual or beyond human resistance]; but God is faithful [to His word—He is compassionate and trustworthy], and He will not let you be tempted beyond your ability [to resist], but along with the temptation He [has in the past and is now and] will [always] provide the way out as well, so that you will be able to endure it [without yielding, and will overcome temptation with joy].* [14] *Therefore, my beloved, run [keep far, far away] from [any sort of] idolatry [and that includes loving anything more than God, or participating in anything that leads to sin and enslaves the soul].* [15] *I am speaking as to wise and sensible people; judge [carefully and thoughtfully consider] for yourselves what I say.*

Prayer

Heavenly Father You are such a forgiving and loving God, thank you for Your mercy. I come to You this day asking for forgiveness of all the sins I have committed against You and Your creation... the sins that I do knowingly and unknowingly. Today, I will no longer be a slave to my iniquities! I ask You to create a clean heart in me right now and renew Your Spirit in me. I ask You to grant me an abundance of Godly Wisdom to understand situations and circumstances that I find myself in; to know how to handle them, how to get away from them, how to speak and act and react when temptation and sin is at my door. Help me to recognize the door of escape that You promised to provide for every temptation that comes my way and Lord allow me to go through that door. Continue to strengthen me in the areas I am strong and build me and strengthen me in the areas of my life that I am weak. Lord, I desire to do what is righteous, Holy Spirit lead and guide my footsteps. Build my faith, that I may be able to faith block everything the enemy throws my direction. Lord put a shield around me that no harm comes to me; help keep my mind and my focus on You and what You have for my life. I Love You with every part of me. In Jesus Name, Amen.

Day 3 – *Intimacy Barrier, Awareness*

A problem why a lot of people do not achieve Intimacy is due to *Awareness* - aware of oneself and what you have to give or share with the other person.

Because of sin that might have been in our life, we feel unworthy to be in relationship with God.

Some of us have experienced something horrible, like some form of abuse. As a result of the abuse, we feel unloved, not beautiful enough, and/or believing something must be ugly about us; therefore, we feel unable or unworthy to go before God.

Others feel like, let the preacher have that relationship or another elder in the church... let that closeness and speaking with God be reserved for those leaders in the church.

God wants you... He desires to be in relationship with you. He wants to talk *with* you. All throughout the Bible, God took the most undesirable and made them great. He took people who had a past: murderers, prostitutes, liars, cheaters, adulterers, fornicators, thieves... even me. God removed the sin and the stain of sin, doubt and unbelief ... and called us friends.

Stop beating yourself up regarding things from your past whether those things are sins, mistakes, or horrible things that have happened to you! God has wiped your slate clean... do you believe yourself higher than God? No, of course not. So if He can wipe your slate clean, so can you. Rebuke the enemy and don't allow him to hold you down over your past.

Even when we are in relationship with God... If we miss reading or spending time with Him, we feel like oh I can't go before His throne. A few readings didn't set you back; stop condemning yourself... that is not

---

of God. Just get back into things with a humble heart. God still loves you!

Scripture

Romans 8:1-3 (NKJV)

There is therefore now no condemnation to those who are in Christ Jesus, who do not walk according to the flesh, but according to the Spirit. [2] For the law of the Spirit of life in Christ Jesus has made me free from the law of sin and death.

Galatians 3:26-29 (KJV)

[26] For you are all sons of God through faith in Christ Jesus. [27] For as many of you as were baptized into Christ have put on Christ. [28] There is neither Jew nor Greek, there is neither slave nor free, there is neither male nor female; for you are all one in Christ Jesus. [29] And if you are Christ's, then you are Abraham's seed, and heirs according to the promise.

Prayer

Lord God, Ruler and Creator of All. Thank You for Your sacrifice and wiping my slate clean. Remove the guilt and shame that I carry and allow Your love and joy and peace to encompass my being. Help me to see my value, being an heir in Your Kingdom. Help me to understand my authority and power in You, and be able to wisely and victoriously operate in Your power. In Jesus Name, Amen.

Day 4 – *Intimacy Barriers, Time and Communication*

We have removed sin from our camp! Now let us explore our next barrier of Intimacy... Time

Our lives in today's world are so preoccupied with so many important things: spouses, children, parents, household things, work, church stuff, school, health, family and friends, ministry, our dreams and goals... plus find time to eat and sleep. We are busy!

Be honest with yourself. How much time are you leaving for God?

When you wake up in the morning, what is the first thing you do... do you grab your phone? What is the last thing you do before you go to sleep? These 2 simple things set the precedent of what is most important to you right now... We must have time for God.

As crazy as this world is, we need time with God. Easier said than done, right? Well, we find time to do other things like eat... we have to make God a priority. What are your hindrances?

Some people choose to wake up a little earlier to spend time with God (praying, reading, studying, praising, worshiping- one or a combination). Others like to wait until before bedtime. Now as for me, I have learned that setting a time just doesn't work. If I miss my scheduled time... then I will say, I can do it tomorrow. Tomorrow turns into the next day then the next... now I'm feeling guilty because I made no time for God. Stop! Do not beat yourself up. Days in my household, with a husband and 3 kids and household things and church stuff, are different every day. When I released myself of a scheduled time, I released the pressure. I spent time with God each day a little different. Some days I had time in the morning, some days at night, some days waiting in the carline at my child's school, some days while I cooked dinner... I got some time.

Another *release the pressure moment* was when I realized spending time with God not only included a special set aside time, but also 24-7 time. My entire day is open to the Lord! I will seek Him first and with all I do... throughout the day I can bust out in song, listen to gospel music in my car, read one scripture/verse before getting out the bed and meditate on that word as much as I can all day, and pray.

Prayer is our Communication with God. In any relationship, there will be failure when there is none or a lack of communication.

Consider this, in a relationship do you say everything that needs to be said at one time, whether that is morning or night? Or do you speak to that person throughout the day? This conversation is the same as with Our Heavenly Father. Yes we have our morning and night time prayers, but the key to communication is to continue it all day. Just have conversation with Him, like you communicate with your best friend.

Have you ever asked God how He is doing? He might begin to share with you the concerns of the world and give you a word to carry to the nations or a particular person. Just make sure that you are not doing anything to stop the 24-7 communication. Ask yourself is my behavior, conversation, or any of my actions breaking up my communication with My Lord, My Savior, My Friend.

Scriptures

1 Thessalonians 5:17 (KJV)
Pray without ceasing.

Psalms 1:2 (KJV)
But his delight is in the law of the Lord; and in his law doth he meditate day and night.

Colossians 4:2 (AMP)
Be earnest and unwearied and steadfast in your prayer [life], being [both] alert and intent in [your praying] with thanksgiving.

Matthew 6:33 (KJV)

But seek ye first of the kingdom of God, and His righteousness and all these things shall be added unto you.

Romans 12:1 (MSG)

[1-2] So here's what I want you to do, God helping you: Take your everyday, ordinary life—your sleeping, eating, going-to-work, and walking-around life—and place it before God as an offering. Embracing what God does for you is the best thing you can do for him. Don't become so well-adjusted to your culture that you fit into it without even thinking. Instead, fix your attention on God. You'll be changed from the inside out. Readily recognize what he wants from you, and quickly respond to it. Unlike the culture around you, always dragging you down to its level of immaturity, God brings the best out of you, develops well-formed maturity in you.

Prayer

Merciful Heavenly Father, I just want to tell You that I Love You. You have been so faithful in everything, my desire is to be faithful to You. Today I understand that from now on my time with You is 24-7. Put a hunger in me for You. Your word says if I hunger and thirst after righteousness, I shall be filled. God fill me. Lord as You fill me up help me begin to discern Your voice and begin to communicate with You clearly throughout the day. You said in Your Word that Your sheep know Your voice, God I am Your follower… I claim the promise of knowing Your voice. As Your voice becomes so recognizable to me continue to build relationship and Intimacy with You. Thank you for granting my request. Beloved, You are mine and I am Yours. In Jesus Name, Amen.

Day 5 − *Intimacy Barriers, Shyness and Game Playing*

In an intimate relationship, if one is too shy to open themselves up to the other person, a barrier will be formed.

Shyness can be defined as a fear or reluctance to be intimate. That person displaying shyness will have to do some serious soul searching on the root of this fear. Have they been hurt before in an intimate relationship, so they are reluctant to be that close to someone again? Have they witnessed relationships go sour when people get too close, so they refuse to allow that to happen them... building a barrier/wall around their heart? Or, they've never seen a real relationship and/or people in their family do not show affection or real intimacy; consequently, they just don't know how.

Another problem is the person trying to be someone they are not. They become stereotypical... let me act like this, or say this, or wear this... instead of just being themselves and let the honesty of the relationship build the relationship. Nothing is worse than falling in love with someone and then realizing that who you fell in love with is not their true self.

These 2 barriers can be related back to God. Sometimes we show fear towards who God is that we don't become intimate. Yes God is All-Powerful and All-Knowing, yet He still wants to talk with you about your day. When you get familiar speaking with God [You are in relationship, you know what your intimate friend sounds like and looks like] then you will know when He begins to lead you to do certain things or tell you when and how to do something.

We might be the only one in our family or a group of close friends who want to know God intimately so we do not have an example of what that looks like. Get you a spiritual mentor (you will know them by their fruits-their character, behavior, actions, reactions, and communication), attend Bible studies, and surround yourself with people who have your common goal- intimacy with God.

Then just come as you are... be yourself. You don't have to come to Him in a preacher's tone, quoting scriptures, or using dignified words. Just open your heart to God... He created you, He knows you, and He will meet you right where you are.

Scriptures

2 Timothy 1:7 (KJV)
For God hath not given us the spirit of fear; but of power, and of love, and of a sound mind.

Romans 8:15-17 (MSG)
15-17 This resurrection life you received from God is not a timid, grave-tending life. It's adventurously expectant, greeting God with a childlike "What's next, Papa?" God's Spirit touches our spirits and confirms who we really are. We know who He is, and we know who we are: Father and children. And we know we are going to get what's coming to us—an unbelievable inheritance! We go through exactly what Christ goes through. If we go through the hard times with Him, then we're certainly going to go through the good times with Him!

Hebrews 4:16a (KJV)
Let us come boldly to the throne of grace

Matthew 6:5-15 (TEV)
When you pray, do not use a lot of meaningless words, as the pagans do, who think their gods will hear them because their prayers are long. Do not be like them. Your Father already knows what you need before you ask Him.

Prayer

Lord God Almighty You are so Wonderful! You are such a Kind and Loving Father! You are All-Powerful and All-Knowing! I Thank You for Your Word and allowing me to mature in this relationship with You. Lord God, rebuke the spirit of fear over my life and I receive the Spirit of Adoption; because I have been adopted as Your child… I now have Your Power in me that destroys fear! I claim and receive power, love, and a sound mind! Thank You for letting me come to You boldly. I am honored that I can be in relationship with You. Continue to let our relationship grow and mature. I look forward to the spiritual heights I can climb with You. In Jesus Name I pray, Amen

Day 6 – *Intimacy Type, Cognitive/Intellectual*

Cognitive or Intellectual – share opinions, ideas, open/comfortable conversation

Picture this, you meet this really great person and now you want to get to know them a little better. You talk all the time – you know their values, goals, what makes them furious, what makes them smile, their likes, and dislikes. You share your thoughts and opinions; you share your goals and your ideas. Your conversation is just amazing!

How can you have a cognitive connection with God? How do you learn his dislikes and likes? How can you have open and comfortable conversation with God? Just like building the cognitive with a person.

Know Him
You want to get to know God... Read His Word, Study His Word! You will read countless stories about what people did to receive blessings, what people did to be cursed. You will learn of the thoughts of God, His teachings, what He has to offer...

The things that God hates –

Proverbs 6:16-19 (KJV)
[16] *These six things doth the Lord hate: yea, seven are an abomination unto him:* [17] *A proud look, a lying tongue, and hands that shed innocent blood,* [18] *An heart that deviseth wicked imaginations, feet that be swift in running to mischief,* [19] *A false witness that speaketh lies, and he that soweth discord among brethren.*

Explanation
You must not find the things God hates as part of your character.

I will be humble; I will tell the truth (or just cover my mouth); I am not hurting someone who is innocent, blameless, naïve, childlike, gullible, pure, harmless; I don't plan to do evil, or scheme how to be sneaky or get over; I am not quick to do something not exemplifying Christ (cursing, drinking, smoking, clubbing, freaking, sexing, stealing, robbing, cheating...); I am not a fake/insincere/made-up witness (you were not involved or not even there as an observer, bystander, or eyewitness so you are just pouring out he said she said gossip spreading lies); I am not causing drama, confusion, and/or trouble in my church or amongst God's people!

You will learn that God is happy when you do His commandments and all of them are based on two –

Mark 12:29-31 (KJV)
[29] And Jesus answered him, The first of all the commandments is, Hear, O Israel; The Lord our God is one Lord: [30] And thou shalt love the Lord thy God with all thy heart, and with all thy soul, and with all thy mind, and with all thy strength: this is the first commandment. [31] And the second is like, namely this, Thou shalt love thy neighbor as thyself. There is none other commandment greater than these.

Explanation
Everything you do should be based on your love for God.
I love God so I am going to do this...I love God so I won't do that...I love God so I will say this...I love God so I won't say that...I love God so I won't go there...I love God so I will treat you like such...I love myself enough that I will only call you what I would call myself or treat you how I treat myself...I love God so I will act like it!

Start really getting in God's Word and studying it, learning of Him. Use the people in the Bible to teach you how God responds to certain situations and behaviors. As you are doing this, continue to have open dialogue with God asking Him to reveal Himself to you and praying about what you are reading to get the revelation needed at that time.

Prayer

Lord God Almighty. Thank you for Your Word. I desire to seek after You and learn of You. Teach me Your ways, show me You. I want to serve You and please You. In my reading time, let Your Word be so clear to me... grant me the wisdom and knowledge and understanding as I read and learn. Give me the gift of discerning of the spirits so I can decipher if a teaching is from You or not; do not allow me to be misled by false teachings. Thank you for giving me this opportunity to know You. In the name of Jesus. Amen

Day 7 – *Intimacy Type,*
Experimental or Intimacy Activity

Experimental or Intimacy Activity – actively involved with each other, maybe saying little of nothing…not sharing thoughts or feelings.

Relating this Intimacy type back to God is making a Spiritual Connection. This can be done in two ways: a ministry service or just being in His presence.

An Experimental Activity/Ministry Service is doing a service for others unto the Lord. Whether it is volunteering at a soup kitchen, cleaning up your church…   You are not actively in conversation with the Lord; however, you are in His presence by actively doing a service unto Him.

An Intimacy Activity is simple to understand when relating it to a close friend or spouse. An example of this activity is when you are just sitting on the couch watching television with your friend or spouse. You are not really talking; you just want to be around each other… just being in each other's presence. The same unto God, you just find yourself sitting in His presence.

My favorite way to sit in the presence of God is to listen to some worship music and just sit on my couch with my eyes closed. Allowing the worship to escort me to the throne of God and just dwell there. Some of you might have a prayer closet, or a special place you speak to God… go there and just relax with your mind focused on our Awesome Father and stay there for a while. You could read a Psalms and then just sit in quietness, meditating on God. In this time God will comfort your heart. He will make His presence aware to you… nothing could be said, but you know that God is with you. You might find yourself at times crying or even worshipping… then if God speaks… Amazing. There is a blessing to just sit in the presence, dwell in the secret place, with God.

After reading the scripture and the prayer, take some time for an Intimacy Activity with The Lord. Just quietly sit with Him and enjoy His presence.

Scriptures

Psalms 91:1 (KJV)

He that dwelleth in the secret place of the most High shall abide under the shadow of the Almighty. [2] I will say of the Lord, He is my refuge and my fortress: my God; in him will I trust. [3] Surely he shall deliver thee from the snare of the fowler, and from the noisome pestilence. [4] He shall cover thee with his feathers, and under his wings shalt thou trust: his truth shall be thy shield and buckler. [5] Thou shalt not be afraid for the terror by night; nor for the arrow that flieth by day; [6] Nor for the pestilence that walketh in darkness; nor for the destruction that wasteth at noonday. [7] A thousand shall fall at thy side, and ten thousand at thy right hand; but it shall not come nigh thee. [8] Only with thine eyes shalt thou behold and see the reward of the wicked. [9] Because thou hast made the Lord, which is my refuge, even the most High, thy habitation; [10] There shall no evil befall thee, neither shall any plague come nigh thy dwelling. [11] For he shall give his angels charge over thee, to keep thee in all thy ways. [12] They shall bear thee up in their hands, lest thou dash thy foot against a stone. [13] Thou shalt tread upon the lion and adder: the young lion and the dragon shalt thou trample under feet. [14] Because he hath set his love upon me, therefore will I deliver him: I will set him on high, because he hath known my name. [15] He shall call upon me, and I will answer him: I will be with him in trouble; I will deliver him, and honor him. [16] With long life will I satisfy him, and shew him my salvation.

Psalms 91 (MSG)

[1-13] You who sit down in the High God's presence, spend the night in Shaddai's shadow, Say this: "God, you're my refuge. I trust in you and I'm safe!" That's right—he rescues you from hidden traps, shields you from deadly hazards. His huge outstretched arms protect you— under

*them you're perfectly safe; his arms fend off all harm. Fear nothing—
not wild wolves in the night, not flying arrows in the day, Not disease
that prowls through the darkness, not disaster that erupts at high noon.
Even though others succumb all around, drop like flies right and left, no
harm will even graze you. You'll stand untouched, watch it all from a
distance, watch the wicked turn into corpses. Yes, because God's your
refuge, the High God your very own home, Evil can't get close to you,
harm can't get through the door. He ordered his angels to guard you
wherever you go. If you stumble, they'll catch you; their job is to keep
you from falling. You'll walk unharmed among lions and snakes, and
kick young lions and serpents from the path. [14-16] "If you'll hold on to me
for dear life," says God, "I'll get you out of any trouble. I'll give you the
best of care if you'll only get to know and trust me. Call me and I'll
answer, be at your side in bad times; I'll rescue you, then throw you a
party. I'll give you a long life, give you a long drink of salvation!"*

Prayer

**Almighty God, Ruler of the Universe, My Strength, My Safety, My
Dwelling Place. God I honor You and adore You. Allow Your Presence
to totally engulf my life. Let me know what Your Spirit feels like, looks
like… is like. As You help me to dwell in Your Presence, fill me up Lord
with Your Spirit… overflow in me. Holy Spirit You are welcome here,
come flood this place, fill the atmosphere. I desire your presence
Lord. Oh I love You Lord. Thank you for the promises You gave me in
Your Word, Psalms 91, keeping me unharmed and protecting me as I
dwell in Your Presence. Let me learn to trust in all those promises. In
Your Son Jesus' Name. Amen**

Day 8 – *Intimacy Type, Emotional Connection*

Emotional Connection –
share feelings/empathize/ aware of emotional state

Spiritual Connection –
have you ever had a conversation with God and asked how He is doing today...God sharing with you his hurts, his people are doing...maybe share something concerning the nation or one particular person that He can use you to help

Think about your relationship with your sweetie. Married couples, think how you behaved when you were dating!

You woke up thinking of them, excited to call and say good morning. You picked out an outfit based on what your sweetie would like to see you wear. Even though you were headed to work or school you made time to talk with, see, or send a message to them.

Throughout your busy day, you couldn't wait to have a break to speak with the love of your life. Daydreaming and just smiling at the mention of his or her name. You are so sprung sending text messages like, just thinking of you baby, or I love you...for the oldies, I'm just calling to say I love you!

People have noticed your glow and ask many questions. Why are you so happy? Who is putting that smile on your face and that swag in your walk? They see the obvious picture you have at your desk, in your locker, or on your phone. You are so proud to show off your baby!!! You are in love!

You also made sure you set aside some time in your day for just the two of you. Then, even though you two had been inseparable (physically, emotionally and/or mentally) all day long, the last voice you heard before you went to bed belonged to your love... Good night baby, I love you. Those of you truly smitten go to sleep with them on the phone.

IS GOD NOT MORE?

Do you wake up thinking of Him? Do you dress yourself with Him in mind? Even though your day is busy with worldly things, you can't begin accomplishing them until you speak to your boo – JESUS!

Are you speaking to Him every moment you get? Are you sending messages throughout the day just to let Him know you are thinking about Him, a thank you, praise, or just I love you Jesus!

Have people noticed something different about you...your behavior, the smile, the way you walk, how you speak, your swag? Is there tangible evidence around you that God is the center of your world? Are you proud to tell others about Jesus?

Is He the last one you speak with before closing your eyes?

You talk, He talks... Open Conversation

Does God deserve that? Our God, My God-My Beloved!

Scriptures

Song of Solomon 5:16 (KJV)
He is altogether lovely. This is my beloved, this is my friend

Daniel 2: 20-22 (KJV)
Blessed be the name of God for ever and ever: for wisdom and might are his: [21] And he changeth the times and the seasons: he removeth kings, and setteth up kings: he giveth wisdom unto the wise, and knowledge to them that know understanding: [22] He revealeth the deep and secret things: he knoweth what is in the darkness, and the light dwelleth with him.

John 15:15 (KJV)

15 Henceforth I call you not servants; for the servant knoweth not what his lord doeth: but I have called you friends; for all things that I have heard of my Father I have made known unto you.

1 Corinthians 2:9-10 (KJV)

9 But as it is written, Eye hath not seen, nor ear heard, neither have entered into the heart of man, the things which God hath prepared for them that love him. 10 But God hath revealed them unto us by his Spirit: for the Spirit searcheth all things, yea, the deep things of God.

Colossians 1:26 (KJV)

26 Even the mystery which hath been hid from ages and from generations, but now is made manifest to his saints:

Prayer

My Beloved, My Friend, My Lord... You continue to be Amazing. I claim my position and relationship with You. Thank You for calling me Your friend. Thank You for sharing Your secrets with me. This relationship between You and I is so beautiful to me, allow me to always stay in this place. Defeat the enemy's plots or schemes that try to remove me from this relationship with You. I am a victorious overcomer because You overcame the world. Help me to walk in my authority and faith as I enjoy and grow in this relationship with You. Take me to new heights and greater levels in You. I love You always. In Jesus' Name. Amen.

Day 9 – *Intimacy Type, Worship (Hebrew words)*

As Christians, we always associate Worship with Praise… hence Praise & Worship in the church. Let's differentiate the two. Praise is a form of thanking God, anything God created can praise Him (Psalm148)… we also worship Him. Worship is intimate.

Throughout God's Word worship is discussed. For today's devotional we are learning the Old Testament Hebrew words for worship: Shachah, Caged, and Abad.

> **Shachah** - *to depress - prostrate in homage*
> **Abad** - *to serve*
> **Caged** - *to prostrate oneself (in homage)*

Shachah or *Caged* – we are familiar with these, a position of worship. Prostrate means to lie prone or stretched out with the face downward or bow very low, in worship or submission. You are prostrate in homage (respect, reverence, deference, service, duty, honor, worship) towards the Almighty God.

> When spending your time with God in prayer, listening to music, sitting in His Presence, or getting overwhelmed in worship service… practice being in the position of worship. It brings a position of submission and honor to God. God will be pleased with your honest position of Worship.

> **Leviticus 9:23-24 (KJV)**
> *And the glory of the Lord appeared to all the people. Fire came out from the presence of the Lord and… when the people saw it; they shouted for joy and fell facedown.*

Abad - this creates another dimension of worship. Your lifestyle, your daily walk with God, your work for Christ – serving Him is worship.

How do you serve God in your daily life? How are you acting and reacting?

How are you treating God's creation... your children, spouse, parents, and coworkers.

Is your communication, how you speak or your gestures, proof that you serve God?

Psalm 100: 2 (KJV)
Serve (Abad) the Lord with gladness

Scriptures

1 Samuel 12:24 (KJV)
[24] Only fear the Lord, and serve him in truth with all your heart: for consider how great things he hath done for you.

Colossians 3:23-24 (AMP)
[23] Whatever you do [whatever your task may be], work from the soul [that is, put in your very best effort], as [something done] for the Lord and not for men,[24] knowing [with all certainty] that it is from the Lord [not from men] that you will receive the inheritance which is your [greatest] reward. It is the Lord Christ whom you [actually] serve.

Prayer

Heavenly Father I am in awe of the works of Your hands. You are a just and merciful God. I worship You with all of me; I bow at Your throne in honor and submission. My desire is to worship you fully. Help me to serve You and in all I do from work to dealing with people... doing as if it was for You. Forgive me for all the times I did not do everything like it was unto You. Thank you for the clarity and knowledge of Your Word. Continue to help me grow in You. In Jesus' Name. Amen

Day 10 – *Intimacy Type, Worship (Greek words)*

We discussed the Hebrew words for worship on Day 8. Let us learn the New Testament, Greek words for worship: *Proskuneo, Sebomai, Latreuo*, and *Therapeuo* (today we will look closer at the latter 3).

> **Sebomai** - to reverence, hold in awe; to adore
>
> **Latreuo** - to render religious service of homage; to minister;
>
> **Therapeuo** - to wait upon menially; one who ministers to another; to adore God; to relieve of disease (same word translated 'cure', 'heal', 'worship')

Sebomai - that comes naturally to us as we think on the awesomeness of God with admiration and adoration, respect and reverence, amazement and awe... This is worshiping God for who He is.

> **Psalms 8 (TLB)**
>
> *O Lord our God, the majesty and glory of your name fills all the earth and overflows the heavens.* [2] *You have taught the little children to praise you perfectly. May their example shame and silence your enemies!*
> [3] *When I look up into the night skies and see the work of your fingers—the moon and the stars you have made—* [4] *I cannot understand how you can bother with mere puny man, to pay any attention to him!*
> [5] *And yet you have made him only a little lower than the angels and placed a crown of glory and honor upon his head.*
> [6] *You have put him in charge of everything you made; everything is put under his authority:* [7] *all sheep and oxen, and wild animals too,* [8] *the birds and fish, and all the life in the sea.* [9] *O Jehovah, our Lord, the majesty and glory of your name fills the earth.*

Let's look closer at the definition of *Latreuo* - to worship, to perform sacred services, to offer gifts, to worship God in the observance of the rites instituted for His worship. The following scriptures are a few examples of how this word of worship is used.

Matthew 4:8-10 (KJV)

[8] Again, the devil taketh him up into an exceeding high mountain, and sheweth him all the kingdoms of the world, and the glory of them; [9] And saith unto him, All these things will I give thee, if thou wilt fall down and worship me. [10] Then saith Jesus unto him, Get thee hence, Satan: for it is written, Thou shalt worship the Lord thy God, and him only SHALT THOU SERVE.

Luke 2:36-37 (KJV)

[36] And there was one Anna, a prophetess, the daughter of Phanuel, of the tribe of Aser: she was of a great age, and had lived with an husband seven years from her virginity; [37] And she was a widow of about fourscore and four years, which departed not from the temple, but SERVED God with fastings and prayers night and day.

Hebrews 12:28 (KJV)

[28] Wherefore we receiving a kingdom which cannot be moved, let us have grace, whereby we may SERVE God acceptably with reverence and godly fear:

In the above scripture examples, we learned the following: Sebomai is worship (bowing to) God, with reverence and godly fear; Then *Latreuo* added a different dimension to our worship, through observing rites (religious ceremonies, rituals)... fasting and praying.

Therapeuo deals with using your hands as worship – healing others from sicknesses, diseases, and demons. Here are a few examples of how *Therapeuo* is used in the Bible:

Matthew 9:35(KJV)

[35] And Jesus went about all the cities and villages, teaching in their synagogues, and preaching the gospel of the kingdom, and HEALING every sickness and every disease among the people.

Luke 6:18 (KJV)

[18] And they that were vexed with unclean spirits: and they were HEALED

Another way to get greater understanding of worship *as Latreuo & Therapeuo*, meditate on the definition they both share, to minister/ministering to someone. When you are ministering to someone: this could be feeding the hungry, clothing someone, sharing your home, praying for the sick, taking care of the widows and orphans... all this is showing how much you adore, worship, God.

How can you incorporate *Sebomai, Latreuo,* and *Therapeuo* into your Intimacy Process with God? Look for ways to perform this worship today. Make yourself do this until it becomes a part of your lifestyle.

Prayer

Heavenly Father, The One and True Living God. You are Lord over my life and the Lord of all! How Excellent is Your Name in all the earth, You are Majestic and Glorious, Sovereign and All-Powerful. I worship you this day in the Beauty of Your Holiness. Forgive me for not completely living a lifestyle of worship. As I am growing in You, help me to grow in my worship... in my fasting, in my service, in my actions and behaviors. Thank you for giving me the opportunity to worship You. I desire to be able to minister to Your people, give me opportunities to do so throughout my day. Let my life be such an example to You that people want to know what is different about me. Continue to shine in me so I can shine for You. Grant me the power and opportunity to be able to bring healing to Your people. I Love You with every part of me. In the Mighty Name of Jesus, Amen.

Day 11 – *Intimacy, Proskuneo*

Proskuneo is a Greek word for *Worship*. It is used in the New Testament and the most used word for worship in the Bible.

Proskuneo - *to kiss, like a dog licking his master's hand; to fawn or crouch to; to prostrate oneself in homage; to kiss forward*

The different definitions for Proskuneo, one sticks out more... to kiss. How can you kiss God?

Let's bring this back to relationships.
- Recall what we have been studying regarding intimacy with God. You met this really great person and you want to get to know them a little better. You talk all the time – you know their values, goals, what makes them furious, what makes them smile, their likes, dislikes... Then you decide to enter into a relationship with this person.
- Now you make sure when you are around your sweetie, your lips are not chapped and your breath is fresh because when you or that person leans in for a kiss, of course with your lips so slightly open...it's amazing!

There are 7 Steps to Kissing God:
1) Know God
2) Relationship
3) Soft Lips
4) Clean Mouth
5) In His Presence
6) Lean In
7) Open Mouth

We have already studied to *Know God* and *Relationship* in this devotional. Let's review those topics from Day 6 and Day 8.

Day 6 Review - Know Him

You want to get to know God... Read His Word, Study His Word! You will read countless stories about what people did to receive blessings, what people did to be cursed. You will learn of the thoughts of God, His teachings, what He has to offer...

Remember you must not find the things God hates as part of your character.

> *I will be humble; I will tell the truth (or just cover my mouth); I am not hurting someone who is innocent, blameless, naïve, childlike, gullible, pure, harmless; I don't plan to do evil, or scheme how to be sneaky or get over; I am not quick to do something not exemplifying Christ (cursing, drinking, smoking, clubbing, freaking, sexing, stealing, robbing, cheating...); I am not a fake/insincere/made-up witness (you were not involved or not even there as an observer, bystander, or eyewitness so you are just pouring out he said she said gossip spreading lies); I am not causing drama, confusion, and/or trouble in my church or amongst God's people!*

You will learn that God is happy when you do His commandments and all of them are based on two, loving God and loving your neighbor as He loves them. Therefore, everything you do should be based on your love for God.

> *I love God so I am going to do this...I love God so I won't do that...I love God so I will say this...I love God so I won't say that...I love God so I won't go there...I love God so I will treat you like such...I love myself enough that I will only call you what I would call myself or treat you how I treat myself...I love God so I will act like it!*

Then, really begin to get in God's Word and study it, learn of Him. Use the people in the Bible to teach you how God responds to certain situations and behaviors. As you are doing this, continue to have open dialogue with God asking Him to reveal Himself to you and praying about what you are reading to get the revelation needed at that time.

Day 8 Review - RELATIONSHIP

Is God Worth More?

Do you wake up thinking of Him? Do you dress yourself with Him in mind? Even though your day is busy with worldly things, you can't begin accomplishing them until you speak to your boo – JESUS!

Are you speaking to Him every moment you get? Are you sending messages throughout the day just to let Him know you are thinking about Him, a thank you, praise, or just I love you Jesus!

Have people noticed something different about you...your behavior, the smile, the way you walk, how you speak, your swag? Is there tangible evidence around you that God is the center of your world? Are you proud to tell others about Jesus?

Is He the last one you speak with before closing your eyes?

You talk, He talks... Open Conversation

Does God deserve that? Our God, My God-My Beloved!

Song of Solomon 5:16 (KJV)
He is altogether lovely. This is my beloved, this is my friend

---

Prayer

Heavenly Father, I am in awe of you the Majesty and Strength in Your Name. The work of Your creation, I just want to worship You. As I continue this journey of Worship, continuing to know You and learn of You and building communication between us, open my spirit to be in such connection with Your Spirit that worship is easy and natural. Allow me to be able to find that place of worship wherever I am and also not to be distracted by anything or anyone that would take me away from this place of worship. I Love You and Honor You forever. In Jesus Name, Amen.

Day 12 – *Intimacy, Proskuneo*

Today we focus on Step 3 of Kissing God – Soft Lips

Soft – Gentle – Meek – Humility
You have to make sure in this relationship with God, you stay humble.

You cannot move those lips to speak as if you are greater than God. Know God is who He is even without you.

The Almighty allows you to do and achieve in all matters; it's never you, always Him, and all for His glory.

It is also an honor and a privilege to be allowed in His presence and in relationship with Him. Therefore, there is a humbling reverence you must enjoy as you cohabitate with His Awesomeness.

> **1 Peter 3:4 (KJV)**
> ...A meek and quiet spirit, which is in the sight of God of great price.

> **James 4:6 (KJV)**
> God resist the proud, but gives grace to the humble.

> **James 4:10 (KJV)**
> Humble yourselves in the sight of the Lord, and He shall lift you up.

Lips
Do not part those lips to be deceitful, cunning, sneaky, or tricky. You should speak truth and have continuous praise coming from your lips!

> *1 Peter 3:10 (KJV)*
> For he that will love life, and see good days, let him refrain his tongue from evil, and his lips that they speak no guile:

Hebrews 13:15 (KJV)

By Him therefore let us offer the sacrifice of praise to God continually, that is, the fruit of our lips giving thanks to His name.

Let's put it all together, creating Soft Lips!

<u>**SOFT LIPS**</u>
TRUTH is your MORAL FIBER
HUMILITY is your CHARACTER
PRAISING GOD is your NATURE

Prayer

Lord God, You alone are God. You are Alpha and Omega. Thank You for Your word. Allow me to have a meek spirit, I am claiming the fruit of meekness in my life. Through the name of Jesus I bind all bad roots in my life that show fruits of deceit, cunning, sneakiness, or trickery. If the root is something in my life that needs healing, Lord grant me the healing in those areas and bring deliverance in my life. I claim in Your Name Jesus the fruit of the Holy Spirit, meekness, and boldly and genuinely and wisely operate in that fruit. Give me good examples and understanding of the fruit as I continue to bear it in my life. In the Name of Jesus, Amen.

Day 13 – *Intimacy, Proskuneo*

Today our focus is on Step 4 of Kissing God – *Clean Mouth*

Baby, you are popping that breath mint, gum, or mint spray in your mouth... You cannot have stinky breath around your love if you want to be kissed.

OUR SOVEREIGN GOD IS TOO HOLY FOR YOUR UNHOLY COMMUNICATION.

A foul mouth is: filthy words, filthy jokes, filthy singing, filthy rapping, and negative talk. Watch what comes out of your mouth!

Communication is more than language, it is your character. Watch the things you say, the gestures you make, the things you do, and the lifestyle you live. This is all your communication. Make sure Jesus can be present in everything you are saying and doing.

Would that not be embarrassing if Jesus was standing right there with you while you are communicating? *... He is...*

Scriptures

Ephesians 4: 29 (KJV)
Let no corrupt communication proceed out of your mouth, but that which is good to the use of edifying, that it may minister grace unto the hearers.

Ephesians 5:1-20 (KJV)
Be ye therefore followers of God, as dear children; And walk in love, as Christ also hath loved us, and hath given himself for us an offering and a sacrifice to God for a sweet smelling savor. But fornication, and all uncleanness, or covetousness, let it not be once named among you, as becometh saints; neither filthiness, nor foolish talking, nor jesting, which are not convenient: but rather giving thanks. For this ye know, that no

whoremonger, nor unclean person, nor covetous man, who is an idolater, hath any inheritance in the kingdom of Christ and of God. Let no man deceive you with vain words: for because of these things cometh the wrath of God upon the children of disobedience. Be not ye therefore partakers with them. For ye were sometimes darkness, but now are ye light in the Lord: walk as children of light: For the fruit of the Spirit is in all goodness and righteousness and truth; Proving what is acceptable unto the Lord. And have no fellowship with the unfruitful works of darkness, but rather reprove them. For it is a shame even to speak of those things which are done in secret. But all things that are reproved are made manifest by the light: for whatsoever doth make manifest is light. Wherefore he saith, Awake thou that sleepest, and arise from the dead, and Christ shall give thee light. See then that ye walk circumspectly, not as fools, but as wise, redeeming the time because the days are evil. Wherefore be ye not unwise, but understanding what the will of the Lord is. And be not drunk with wine wherein is excess; but be filled with the Spirit; Speaking to yourselves in psalms and hymns and spiritual songs, singing and making melody in your heart to the Lord; Giving thanks always for all things unto God and the Father in the name of our Lord Jesus Christ; Submitting yourselves one to another in the fear of God.

1 Peter 15-16 (KJV)
But as He which hath called you holy, so be ye holy in all manner of conversation; because it is written, Be ye holy; for I am holy.

Prayer

Lord, All Merciful and Forgiving God, Thank You for Your saving power, for being my Savior. Forgive me for all my corrupt communication, my talk, my gestures, the things I do, my lifestyle... Wash me with hyssop, create in me a clean heart and renew Your right Spirit in me. Remove all temptation, my desire for foul communication and joking. Continue to show my holiness and growth in You. Thank You for Your grace and mercy in Jesus Name, Amen.

Day 14 – *Intimacy, Proskuneo*

Today we focus on Step 5 of Kissing God – *In His Presence*

You know God, you and Him are in a relationship, you are drenched in humility, your communication is holy...you are ready.

Now you are prepared and anticipating the KISS. In order to kiss someone you must be in their (physical) presence.

Hebrews 4:16a (KJV)
Let us therefore come BOLDLY unto the throne of grace,

When Jesus died and rose, He tore the veil that permitted us from getting to the holy of holies...Now you may boldly enter where God sits on His throne.

Mark 15:37-38 (KJV)
And Jesus cried with a loud voice, and gave up the ghost.
And the veil of the temple was rent in twain from top to bottom.

Hebrews 10:19 (KJV)
Having therefore, brethren, boldness to enter into the holiest by the blood of Jesus,

Prayer

Lord Almighty God!! You are so Holy. I ask that You remove any obstacles, anything that would hinder me from coming into total oneness and having an intimate exchange with You... My Heavenly Father, Jesus, and Holy Spirit I desire to be so close to You. I praise You, I honor You, I exalt You, I adore You, I worship You. *(Speaking in tongues might manifest here or would be appropriate.)* **Holy Spirit I ask You to help me pray and lead me to the Throne Room, lead me now into the Holy Place, the Holy of Holies. I come boldly and humbly Lord God, Thank You for welcoming me. Oh how I love You. Keep me focused on You, Your Voice, and Your Presence. Please do not hide Your face from me. At this moment, let me experience a closer encounter with You. In Jesus Name. Amen.**

Day 15 – *Intimacy, Proskuneo*

Today we focus on Step 6 of Kissing God – Lean In

Understanding this step, we must look at lean in three different ways: Lean In, Lean Into and Lean.

LEAN IN

- to incline or press into something; have to lean in a little in the wind so you won't be knocked over

You are in the All-Powerful God's Presence; you must *LEAN IN* or be knocked over. Leaning In is a movement of your body that presses you closer to God (raised hands, stretched out arms, dancing). Keep Leaning In, keep pressing until something happens.

Psalms 63:2 (KJV)
I have seen you in the sanctuary and beheld your power and glory.

2 Samuel 6:16, 21-22 (KJV)
...King David leaping and dancing before the Lord...
It was before the Lord who chose me...He appointed me
I will celebrate before the LORD. I will become even more undignified than this, and I will be humiliated in my own eyes.

Nehemiah 8:6 (KJV)
Ezra praised the Lord, the great God; and all the people lifted their hands and responded, "Amen! Amen!" Then they bowed down and worshiped the LORD with their faces to the ground.

LEAN INTO IT

- in the Urban Dictionary the phrase means to say or do something to the extreme, to do it big.

Getting to His face you must *LEAN INTO IT*, do it big (BOLD).

Ephesians 3:12 (KJV)

In whom we have boldness and access with confidence by the faith of Him.

LEAN

- to incline the weight of the body as to be supported; rely for assistance or support or inspiration.

LEAN on Him for support while relying totally on Him to hold you up (vulnerable).

Psalms 119:117 (KJV)

Hold thou me up, and I will be safe: and I will have respect unto thy statutes continually.

Prayer

Lord God I lift my hands to You, no other God before You. Thank You for this moment to Lean In to You. You are my support, You are my Strength, You are my Safety. I am coming to You through the authority of Your Son and at this moment my worship is big in Your eyes… You see me, You see my worship. Wherever I am allow me to worship and honor You and not be embarrassed or ashamed or worried what spectacle I make, for our relationship is personal and my worship is for real. I Love You and Adore You. In Jesus Name, Amen.

Day 16 – *Intimacy, Proskuneo*

Today we focus on Step 7 of Kissing God – *Open Mouth*

In a kiss, your mouth is open for two reasons: to fill and to be filled.

To Fill

Proskuneo is compared to a dog licking its master. The dog is using its tongue to kiss the master; physically showing excitement, thrill, safety, and love.

You must fill God's presence with adoration. This is achieved by using your tongue in words or songs. I'm happy to be in Your Presence, Lord I adore You, There is safety with You, Lord You're Amazing, You Are Awesome, How I Love You..."

Psalms 18:1-3 (KJV)
I will love thee, O Lord, my strength. The Lord is my rock, and my fortress, and my deliverer; my God, my strength, in whom I will trust; my buckler, and the horn of my salvation, and my hightower.

Psalms 8:1 (KJV)
O Lord our Lord, how excellent is thy name in all the earth! Who has set thy glory above the heavens.

Psalms 29:2 (KJV)
Give unto the Lord the glory due unto His name; worship the Lord in the beauty of holiness.

To Be Filled

Our Lord will fill you with His Adoration. God is Alpha and Omega, everything you have ever needed or desired is in Him (and it is an abundant, never-ending supply).

He is Jesus, the one who by His stripes you are healed; you will find healing in every aspect of your life...physical, emotional, mental. Jesus also overcame the world, you will find victory. He rose with all power, that power lives in you!

He is the Holy Spirit. You will be filled with His Spirit. You may receive a word of wisdom, a word of knowledge, faith, begin to heal, perform miracles, begin to prophesy, discern the spirits, start speaking tongues, and/or interpret the tongues.

God will fill you with Himself.
Romans 15:13 (KJV)
Now the God of hope fill you with all joy and peace in believing, that ye may abound in hope, through the power of the Holy Ghost .

1 Samuel 10:6a (KJV)
And the Spirit of the Lord will come upon thee, and thou shall prophesy

Acts 2:4 (KJV)
And they were all filled with the Holy Ghost, and began to speak in other tongues, as the Spirit gave them utterance.

Psalms 81:10b (KJV)
Open your mouth wide and I will fill it.

You have followed the steps and have Kissed God!
PROSKUNEO!
How Beautiful it is to Kiss the Face of God!

Song of Solomon 5:10-16 (KJV)
His mouth more sweet: yea, HE IS ALTOGETHER LOVELY.
THIS IS MY BELOVED, AND THIS IS MY FRIEND

When *Proskuneo* is complete,

Our Sovereign God is filling you and the atmosphere;

You cannot help but to do every part of *Proskuneo*....

To Crouch, Bow, Prostate Yourself...WORSHIP

Prayer of Worship

I am standing in His Presence

I am dancing, and worshiping

Oh adoring, and reverencing

Humbly and Boldly

I am Kissing Your Face God

Oh I'm so honored, that Your Awesomeness

Would allow me, in Your Presence

Oh I'm so humbled, that Your Holiness

Would allow me, to be so Intimate

I am Kissing Your Face God

My Beloved, Rose of Sharon

Lilly in the Valley, Altogether Lovely

I am My Beloved's, My Beloved is Mine

My God, Jesus Christ

I am Kissing Your Face God

The above prayer includes the lyrics of the song
Kissing The Face of God by Monique Gittens, MoWorship MoGospel
... Coming Soon...

I pray this journey truly blessed you.

I pray you developed a deeper desire to become closer with Our Lord.

I pray you accomplished another level of Intimacy with God.

MoWorshipMoGospel ~ © 2014,2019

Website: www.moworshipmogospel.com
Instagram: @moworshipmogospel
Facebook: MoWorship MoGospel

Tell MY People I AM Coming Back

LIVE FULFILLED
Empowered In Your Purpose, Authoritative In Your Doings, Receiving All The Promises Of God

Made in the USA
Columbia, SC
12 August 2020